CHEROKEE STYLE DOUBLE WALL BASKET

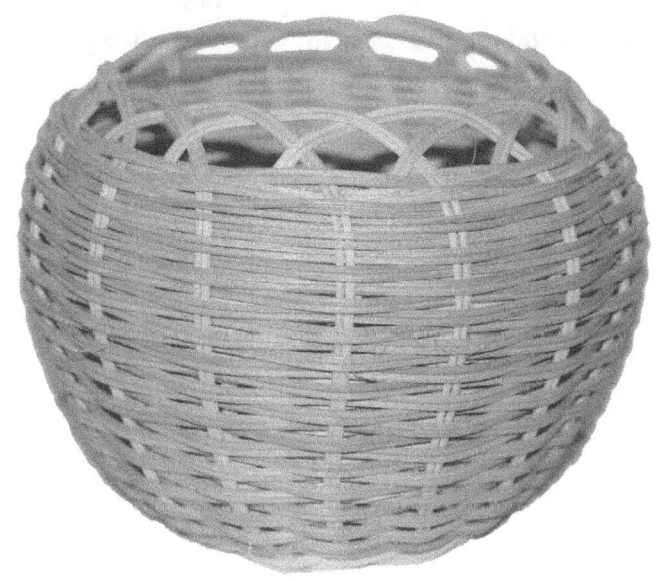

©2006 By Gerald L Findley
Hermon, New York

1

INTRODUCTION

The Cherokee double wall basket is a wicker plaited basket. The design was created by the Oklahoma (Western) Cherokees when they were removed from North Carolina to Oklahoma. The traditional basket is woven of honeysuckle or buckbrush. For a contemporary look, many weavers use round reed for their baskets.

Colored reeds can be used to create patterns of color within various parts of the basket and to enhance the contrast between the various parts of the basket.

The use of different weaving techniques can change the texture of the weave of the basket. While there are numerous weaving patterns that could be used, only four basic patterns are included in this book: single rod, double rod, twining, and open work.

CONTENTS

STARTING A BASKET

The following instructions are for starting a basket that uses the same sized reed for the spokes and the weavers.

The bottom of the basket is the foundation on which a basket is built, so it is important that the bottom is neatly woven.

Each spoke of the finished basket will be composed of two reeds. In these instructions the finished bottom will have a total of 15 spokes.

MATERIALS
Cut the following lengths of #2 or #3 reed.

7 ------------ 32 inch reeds for spokes
16 ---------- 16 inch reeds for spokes
weavers --- total about 150 feet of reed

PROCEDURE
Soak the long spokes and several weavers in warm water for about 5 minutes. Then follow the instructions given in the following diagrams.

IMPORTANT
The weaver should **NOT** be pulled into place but should be firmly pressed into place. Pulling the weaver in place will bend the spokes and distort the shape of the basket.

[STEP 1] Place a group of 3 long spokes across a group of 4 long spokes.

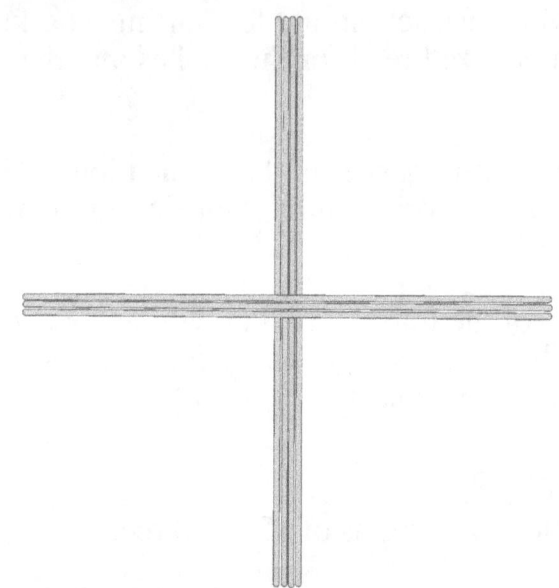

[STEP 2] Start the first weaver.

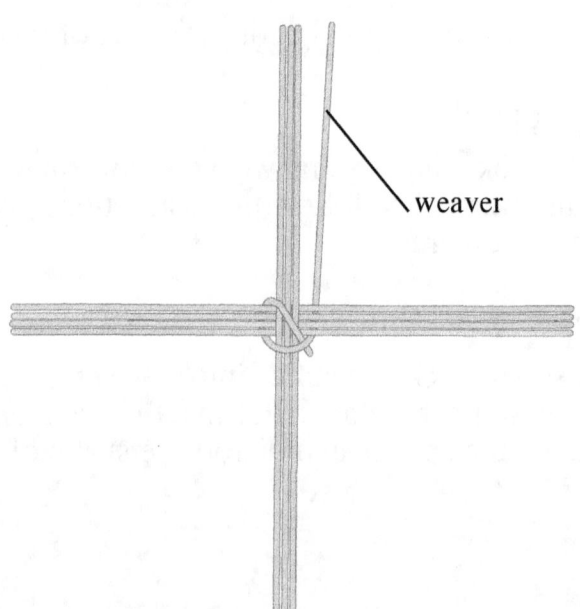

weaver

[STEP 3] Bind the two sets of spokes together. Take 4 or 5 turns.

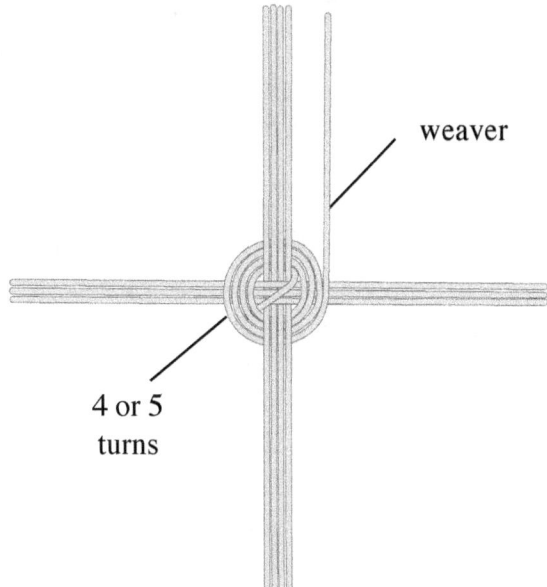

weaver

4 or 5
turns

[STEP 4] Separate the spokes into seven groups with 2 reeds in each group.

[NOTE] An odd number of two reed spokes must be maintained throughout the work.

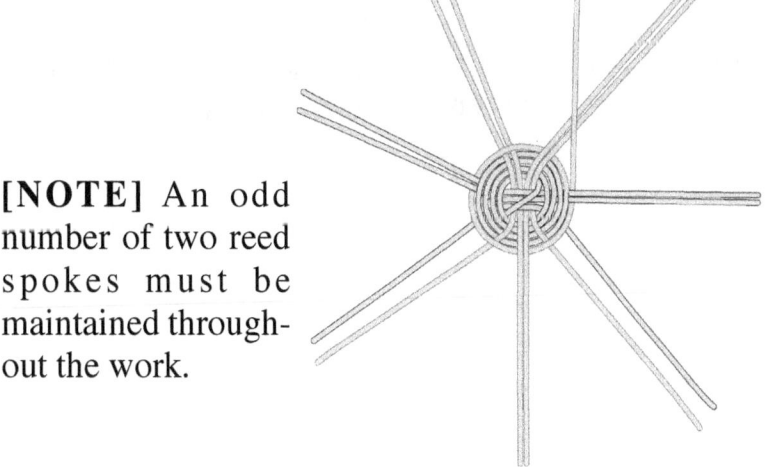

[STEP 5] Weave another 8 to 12 turns.

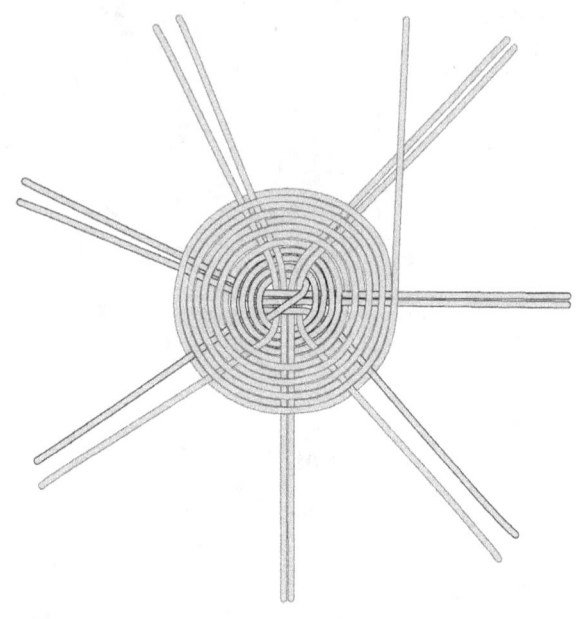

[NOTE] ADDING NEW WEAVERS

As each weaver runs out, a new weaver must be spliced in. The following diagrams illustrate the procedure.

[Step 1] While holding the previous weaver in place, loosely insert new weaver.

[Step 2] Press new weaver firmly in place.

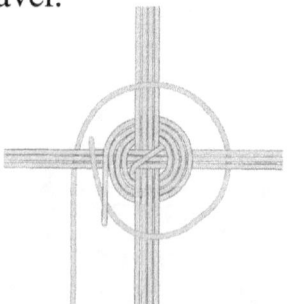

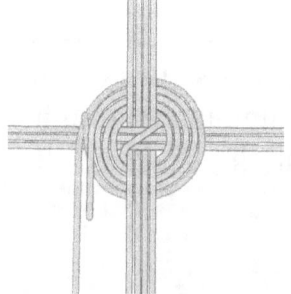

[STEP 6] Insert one short spoke to the outside of each pair of the two-reed spokes. This results in enough reeds to make 14 two-reed spokes.

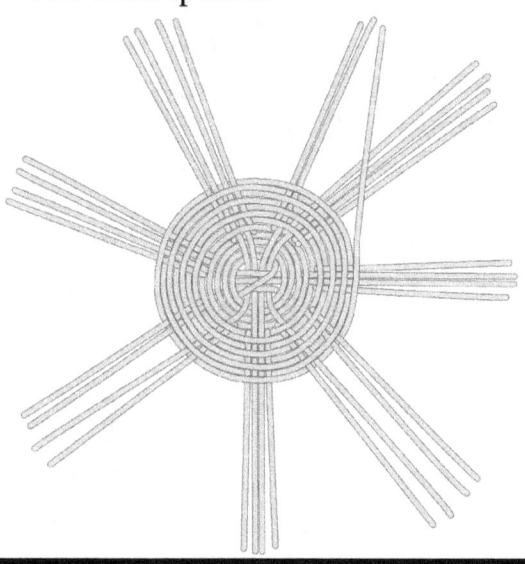

[NOTE] Cont.

[Step 3] Continue to weave.

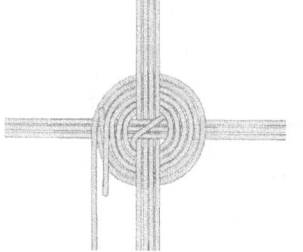

[Step 4] Cut off the ends of the weavers at the site of the splice.

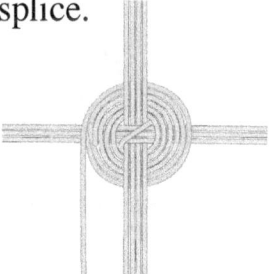

[NOTE] The cutoff ends of the splice should be hidden. On the bottom and the inside wall of the basket the cutoff ends should be toward the outside of the finished basket. On the outside wall the cutoff ends should be toward the inside of the finished basket.

[STEP 7] An additional two short spokes are needed to maintain the odd number of two-reed spokes. Insert two additional spokes as shown. When finished there will be enough reeds to make 15 two-reed spokes.

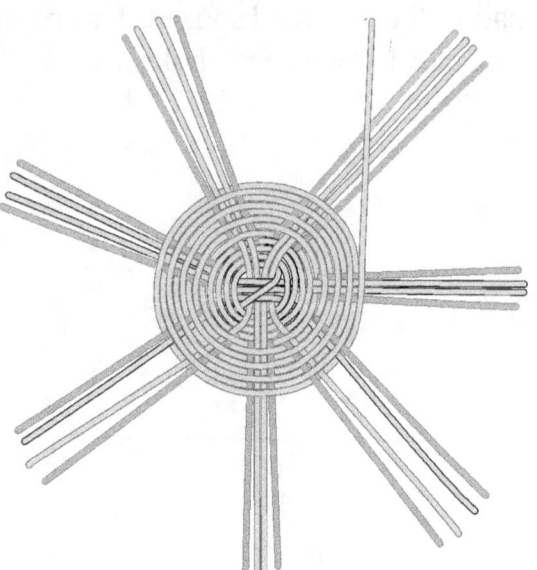

[STEP 8] Separate the spokes into 15 two-reed spokes.

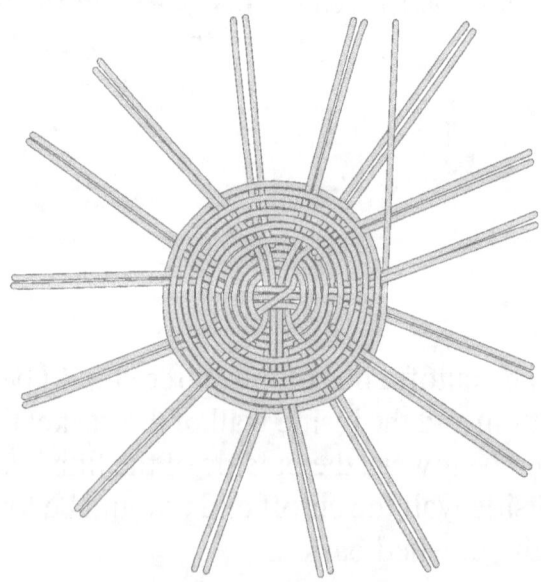

[STEP 9] Weave 5 to 8 more turns.

[NOTE] As these turns of the weaver are added, the spaces between the spokes must be evened out.

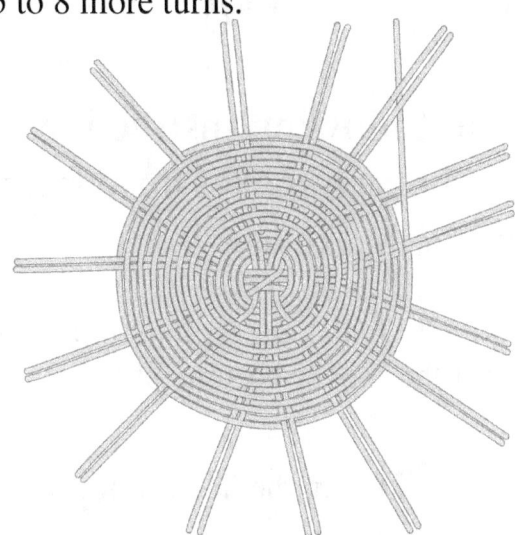

[NOTE] To make a larger basket, a larger bottom is needed. Make a larger bottom by adding additional short spokes. The additional spokes are inserted as shown below.

[NOTE] Be sure to maintain an odd number of spokes.

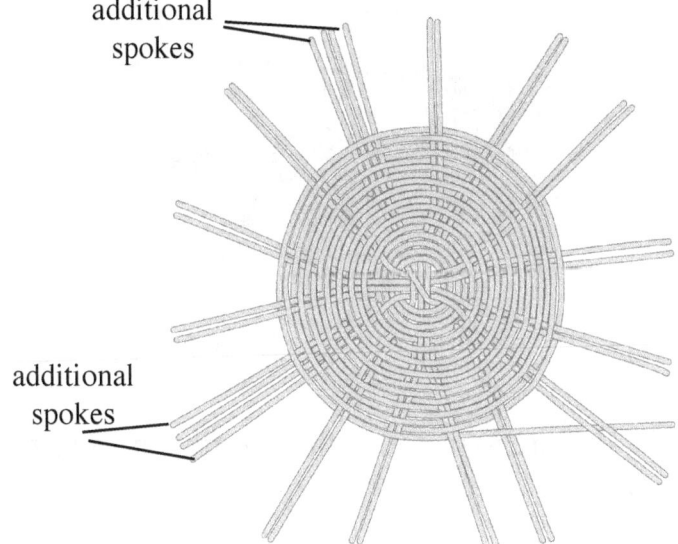

additional spokes

additional spokes

INSIDE WALL

The following instructions are for turning the bottom spokes up to form the inside wall of the basket.

[STEP 1] Soak the bottom of the basket in warm water until the spokes become pliable.

[STEP 2] Turn the first set of spokes upward.

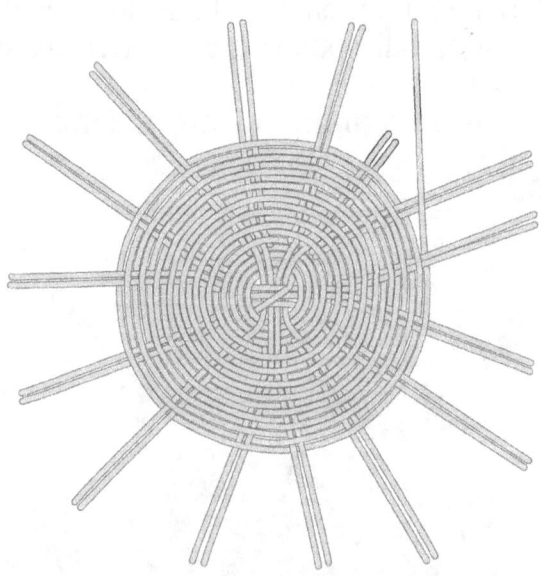

[NOTE] Be sure to maintain the over/under pattern of the weaving.

[STEP 3] Press the weaver firmly in place against the up turned spoke.

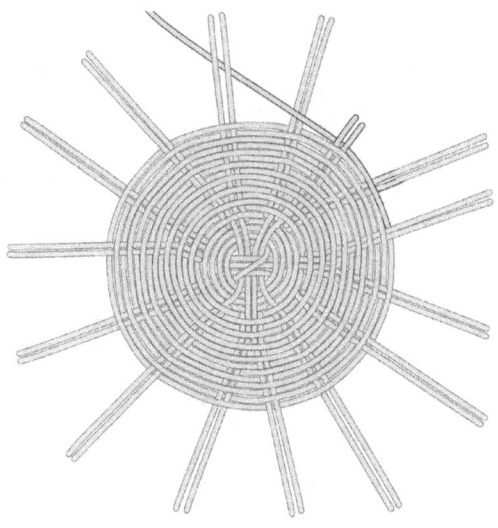

[STEP 4] Turn the third set of spokes up and press the weaver in place.

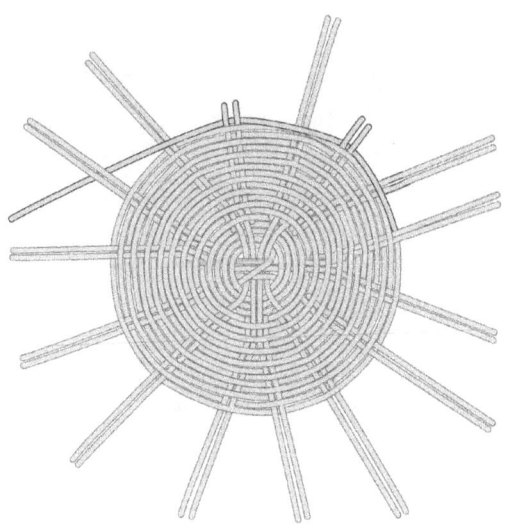

[STEP 5] Continue to work around the bottom of the basket turning every other spoke up and pressing the weaver firmly in place.

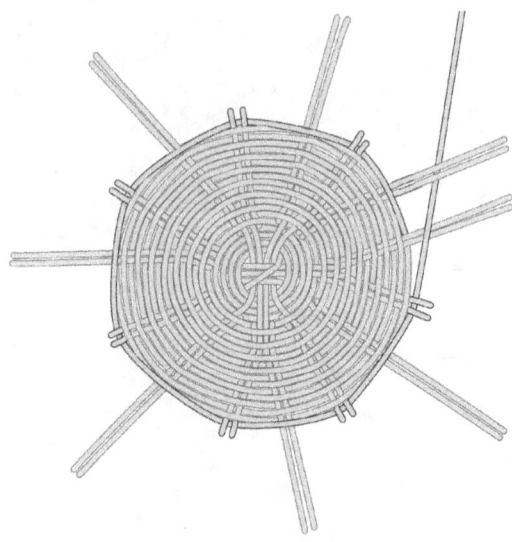

[STEP 6] Start the second round of the wall by continuing to turn up every other spoke and pressing the weaver firmly in place.

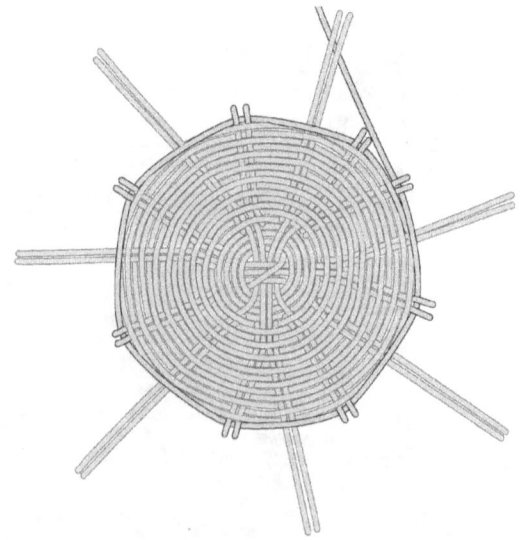

[STEP 7] Complete the second round of the wall by turning up the remaining spokes and pressing the weaver firmly in place.

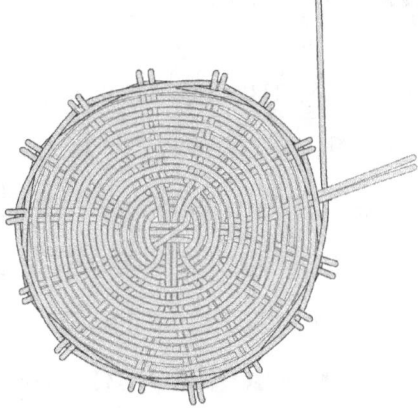

[STEP 8] Complete the inside wall of the basket.

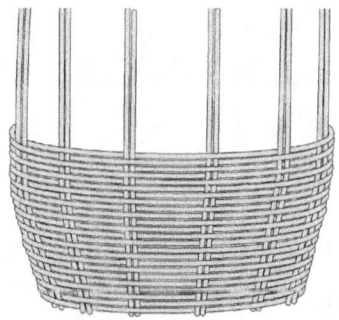

[NOTE] The shape of the basket wall is controlled by increasing and decreasing the diameter of the basket wall.

To increase the diameter of the basket wall, slightly increase the spacing between the spokes.

To decrease the diameter of the basket wall, slightly decrease the spacing between the spokes.

TOP PATTERN 1 AND OUTSIDE WALL

The following instructions are for turning the wall spokes down to form the top and outside wall of the basket. In this set of instructions, each set of spokes goes in front of the adjacent set of spokes, then behind the next set of spokes and finally down the outside of the basket.

[STEP 1] Soak the top of the basket in warm water until the spokes become pliable.

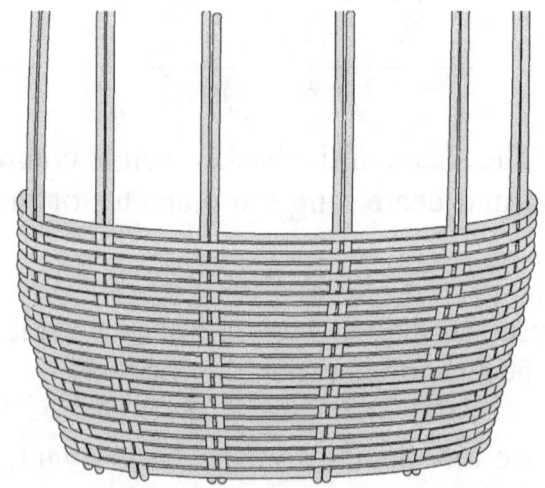

[STEP 2] Weave the first set of spokes to the outside of the adjacent set of spokes then behind the next set of spokes and then turn them down the outside of the basket.

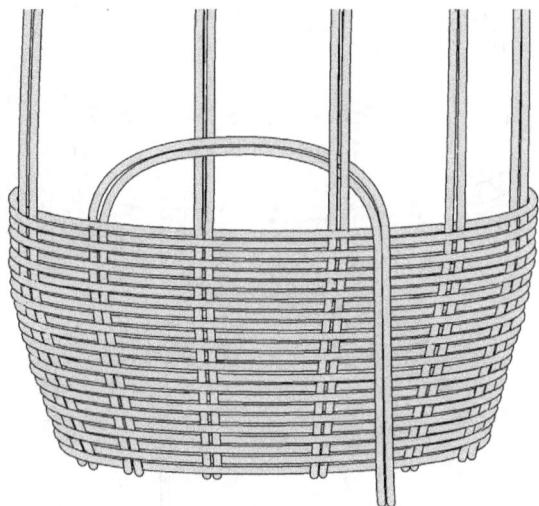

[STEP 3] Repeat step 2 with the adjacent set of spokes.

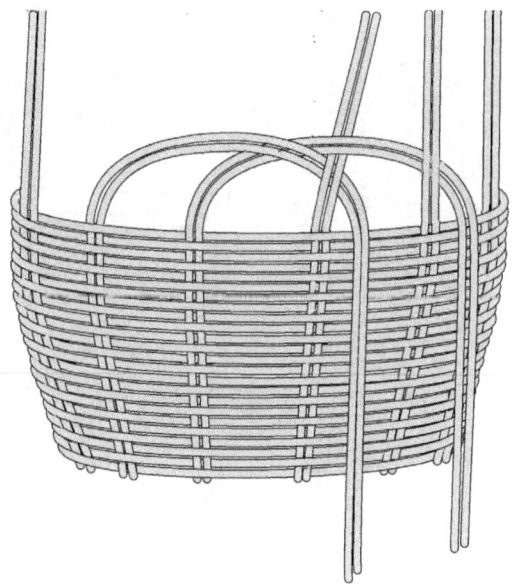

[STEP 4] Repeat step 2 with the next set of spokes.

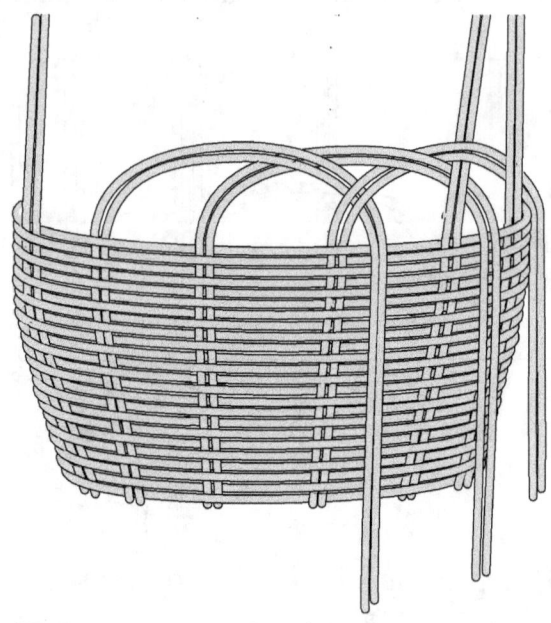

[STEP 5] Repeat step 2 with the remaining sets of spokes.

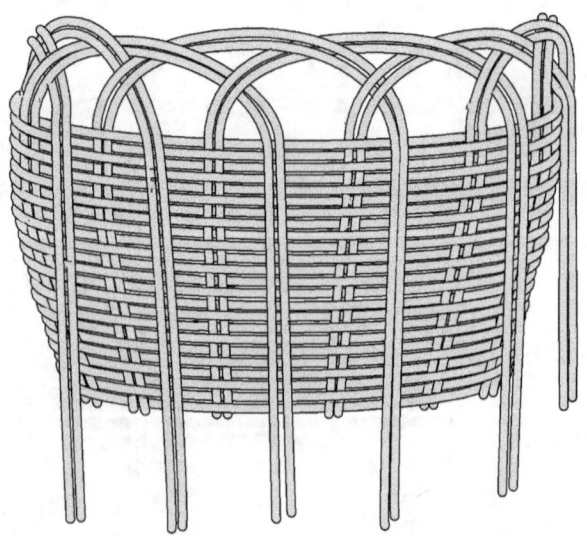

[STEP 6] Insert a new weaver.

new
weaver

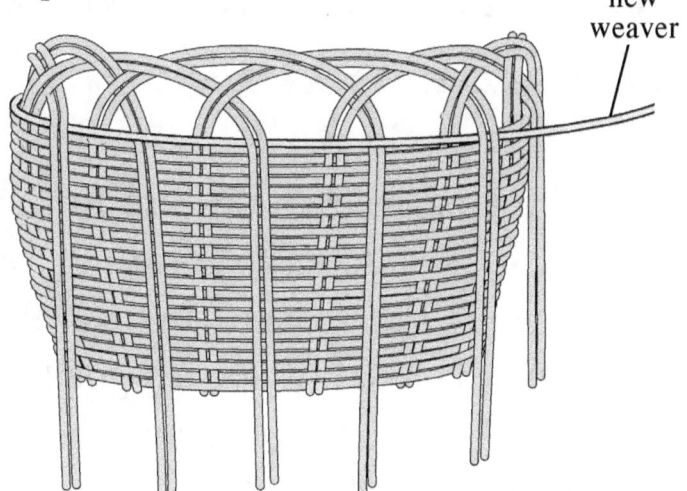

[NOTE] To change the texture of the outside wall, different weaving techniques can be used (see page 30).

[STEP 7] Weave the outside wall.

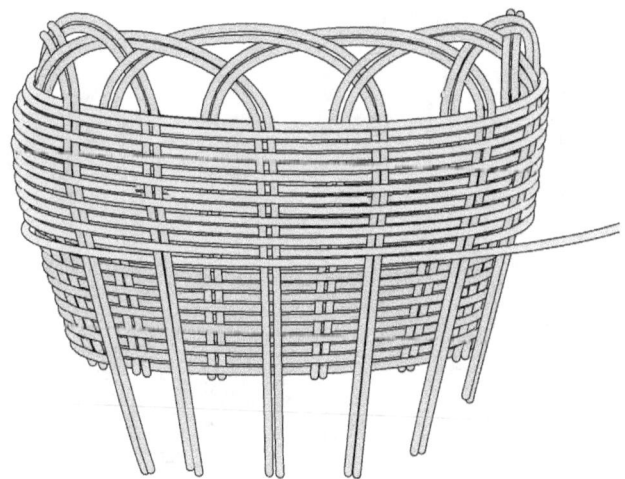

[NOTE] As the outside wall is woven, its shape is controlled by pressing the spokes and weavers firmly against the inside wall.

TOP PATTERN 2 AND OUTSIDE WALL

The following instructions are for turning the wall spokes down to form the top and outside wall of the basket. In this set of instructions, each set of spokes goes behind the adjacent set of spokes and then down the outside of the basket.

[**STEP 1**] Soak the top of the basket in warm water until the spokes become pliable.

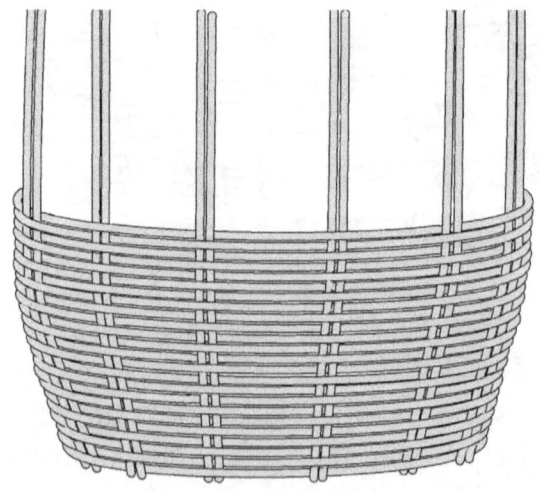

[STEP 2] Weave the first set of spokes to the inside of the adjacent set of spokes and then turn them down the outside of the basket.

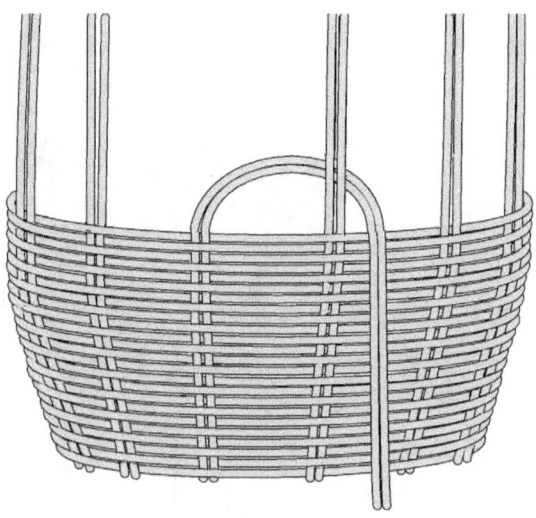

[STEP 3] Repeat step 2 with the adjacent set of spokes.

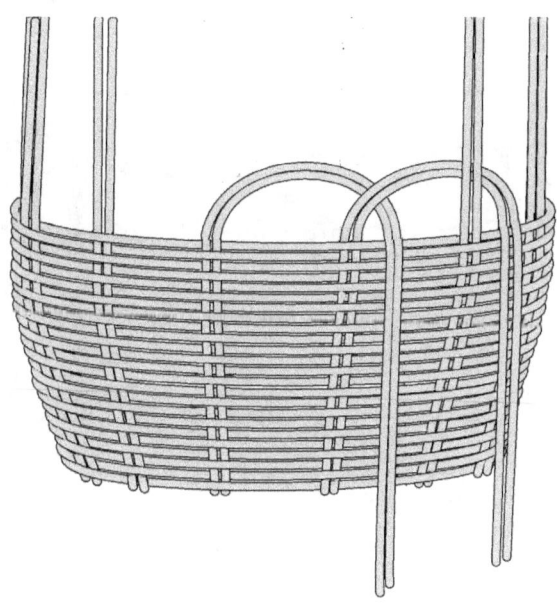

[STEP 4] Repeat step 2 with the next set of spokes.

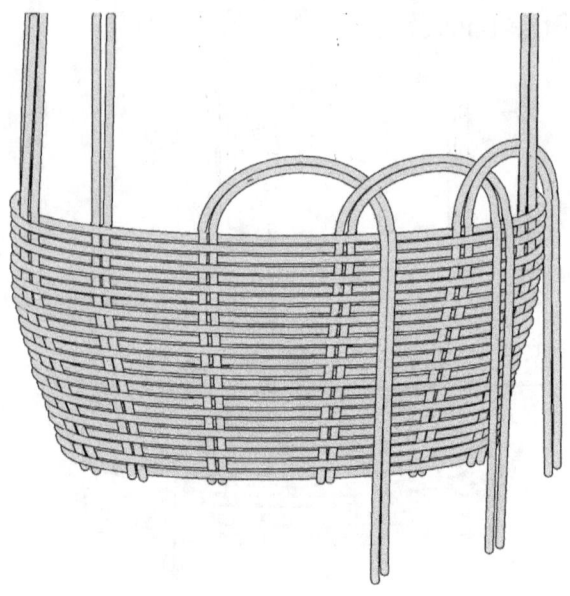

[STEP 5] Repeat step 2 with the remaining sets of spokes.

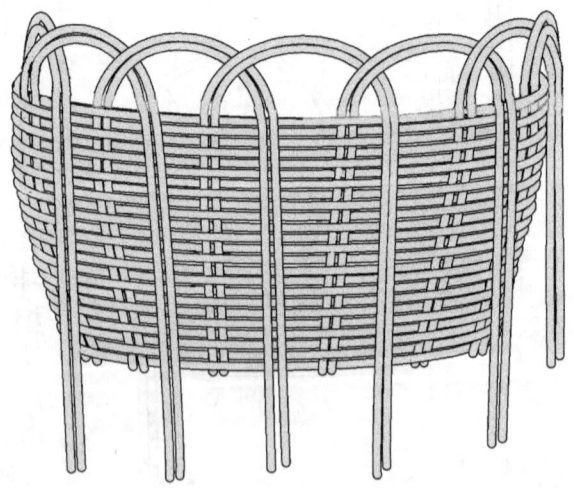

[STEP 6] Insert a new weaver.

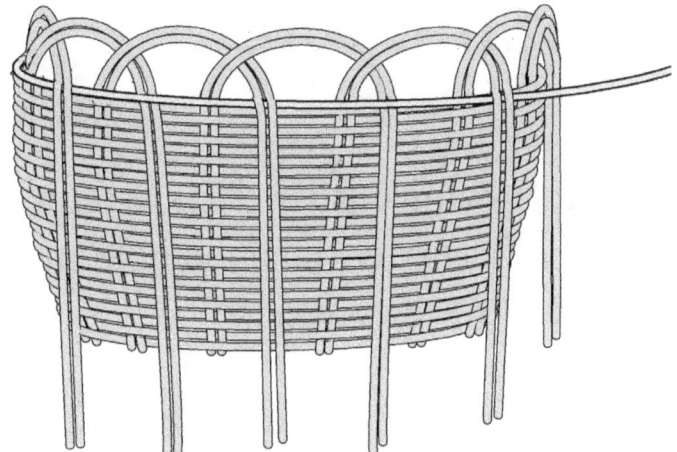

[NOTE] To change the texture of the outside wall, different weaving techniques can be used (see page 30).

[STEP 7] Weave the outside wall.

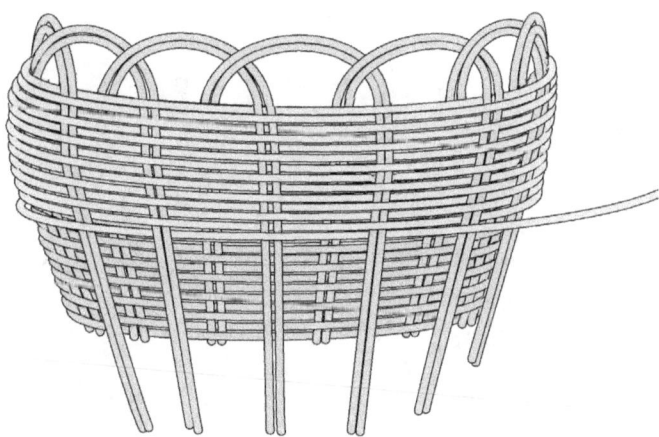

[NOTE] As the outside wall is woven, its shape is controlled by pressing the spokes and weavers firmly against the inside wall.

FINISHING BOTTOM AND OUTSIDE WALL

The following instructions are for turning the spokes up to finish the bottom and outside wall of the basket.

[STEP 1] Soak the bottom of the basket in warm water until the spokes become pliable.

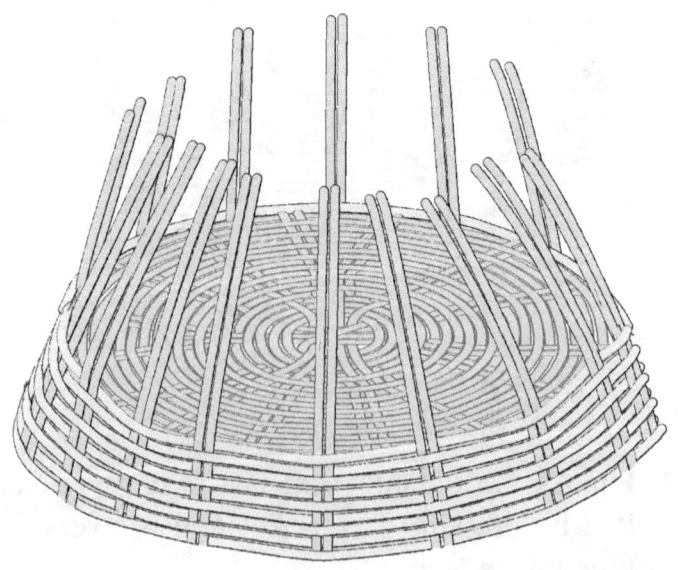

[STEP 2] Weave the first set of spokes to the outside of the adjacent set of spokes then behind the next set of spokes.

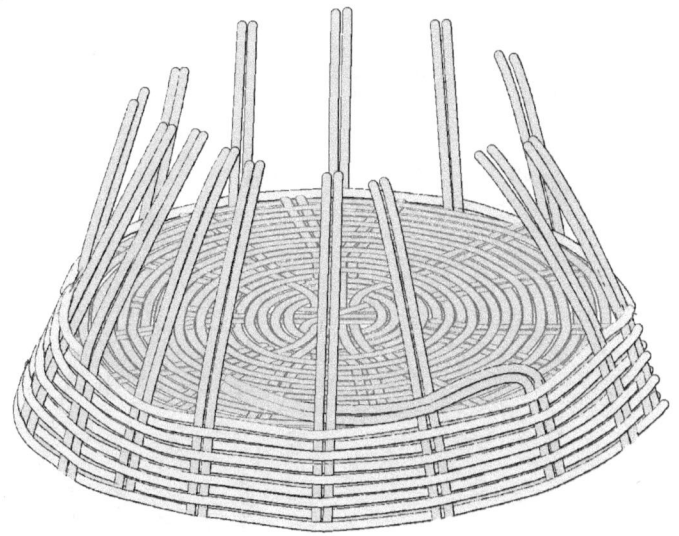

[STEP 3] Cut off the ends of the turned up spokes just past the last set of spokes.

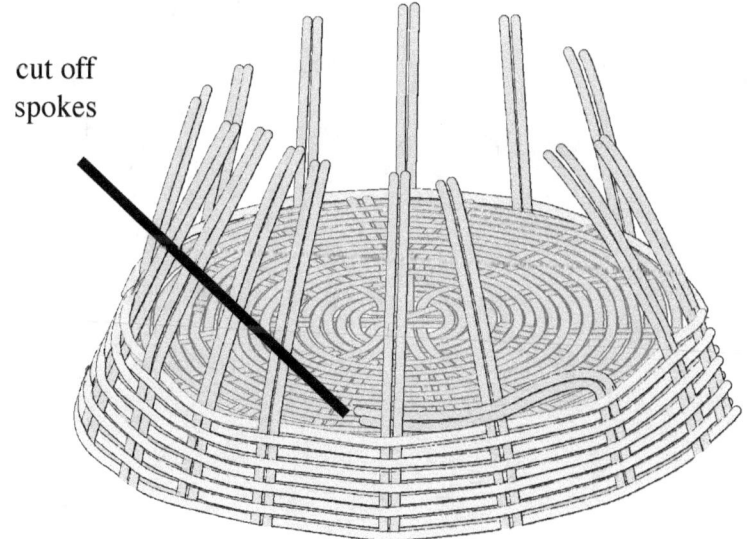

cut off spokes

[STEP 4] Repeat steps 2 and 3 with the adjacent set of spokes.

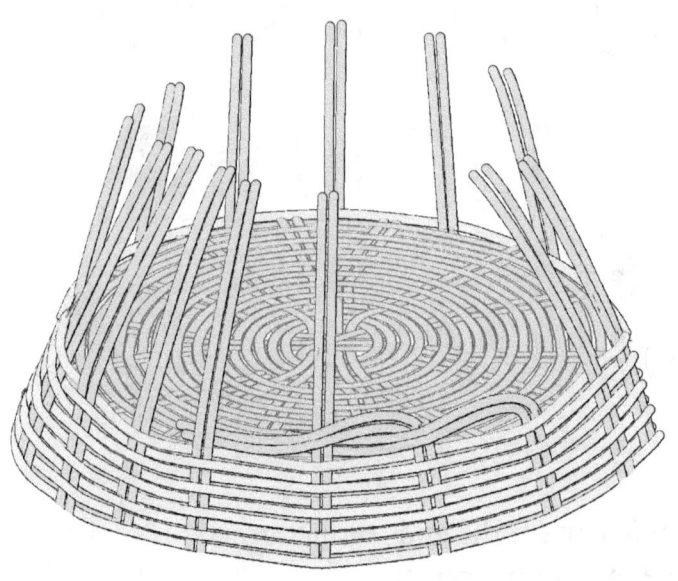

[STEP 5] Repeat steps 2 and 3 with the remaining sets of spokes.

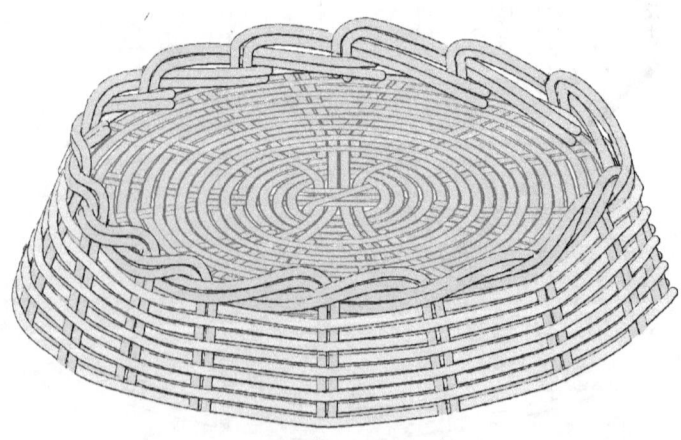

DYEING REED

The addition of colored reeds can be used to create patterns of color within the various parts of the basket and to enhance the contrast between the various parts of the basket.

A variety of natural earthy looking colors can be obtained by applying wood stain to the reed. A good way to do this is to wipe the stain onto the reed with a small pad made out of soft cloth that has been dipped in the stain. Be sure to wear rubber gloves and old clothing while staining the reed using this method.

Brighter and more contemporary looking colors can be obtained by using commercial dye products such as Rit dye. First, soak the reed in water until it is pliable. Prepare the dye bath by following the directions that come with the dye package. Then gently simmer the reed in the dye bath for 1/2 hour or longer. The longer the reed remains in the dye bath the darker the color. When the desired shade of the color is reached, set the dye by rinsing the reed in a solution of half vinegar and half water.

Natural materials can also be used for adding color to the reed. Directions can be found in a variety of books on hand weaving and spinning. Follow the direction for dyeing cotton or linen cloth when using natural dyes.

WARNING! Because of the toxic nature of many dye products, once a pan has been used as a dye pot it should never be used for preparing food.

TEXTURE OF WEAVE

The use of different weaving techniques can change the texture of the weave of the basket. While there are numerous weaving patterns that could be used. only four are included in this book: single rod, double rod, twining, and open work. As you gain experience you may wish to try other weaving patterns.

SINGLE ROD WEAVING

Single rod weaving is done by weaving a single weaver in an over under pattern through the spokes of the basket. This technique is used throughout the basic instructions in the front of this book.

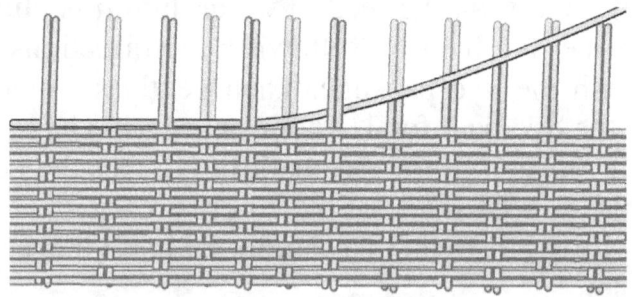

Using contrasting colors for the spokes and the weavers produces a change in the appearance of the single rod weave.

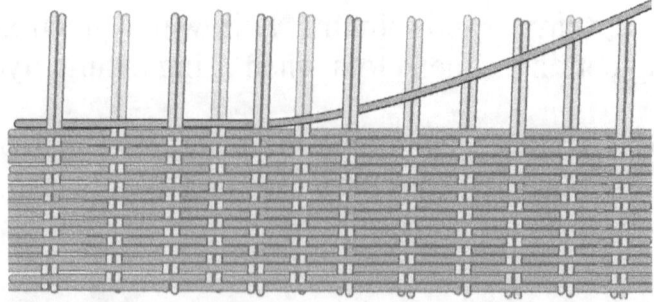

DOUBLE ROD WEAVING

Double rod weaving is done by weaving two parallel weavers in an over under pattern through the spokes of the basket.

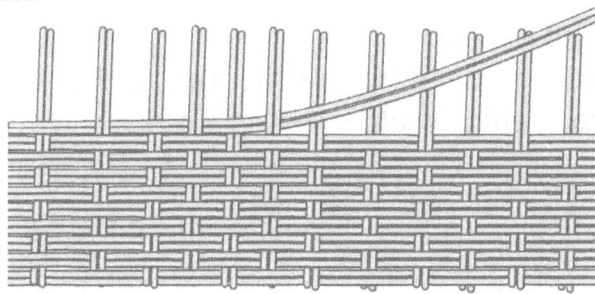

Using contrasting colors for the spokes and the weavers produces a change in the appearance of the double rod weave.

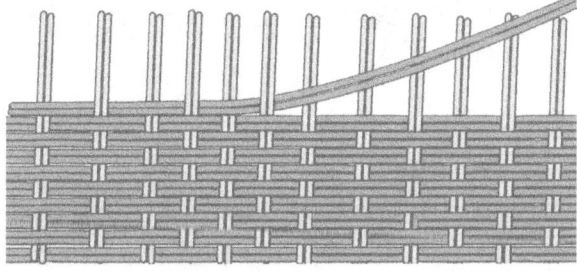

Another change in the appearance of the double rod weave can be produced by using contrasting colors for the two weavers.

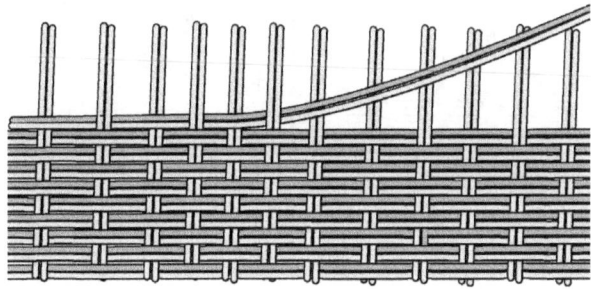

TWINING

Twining is a method of weaving with two rods (reeds) where the rods twist around each other between each set of spokes.

[STEP 1] Twining.
Twining is started by inserting two reeds. One reeds is inserted behind each of two spokes.

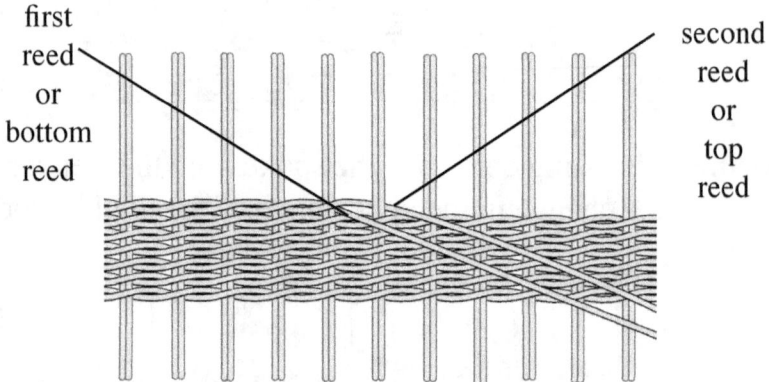

first reed or bottom reed

second reed or top reed

[STEP 2] Twining.
The first reed is taken over the spoke next to it and then under the next spoke. Notice that the first reed passes over the second reed and that the second reed is now in the bottom position.

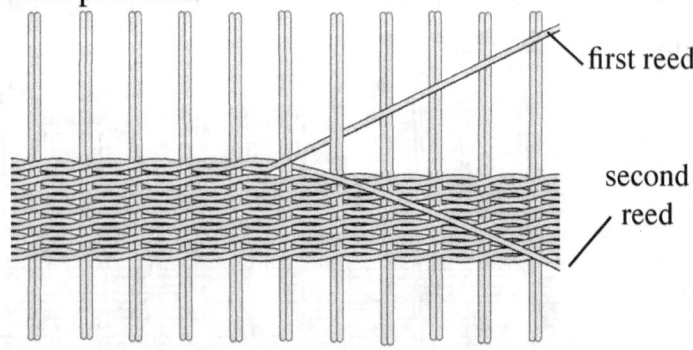

first reed

second reed

[STEP 3] Twining.

The first reed is then pushed into place.

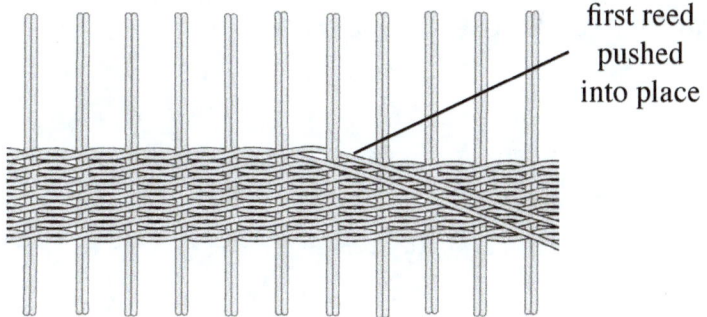

first reed
pushed
into place

[STEP 4] Twining.

Continue weaving by repeating steps 2 and 3 with each new bottom reed.

NOTE

A diagonal or spiral effect can be added by using reeds of contrasting colors.

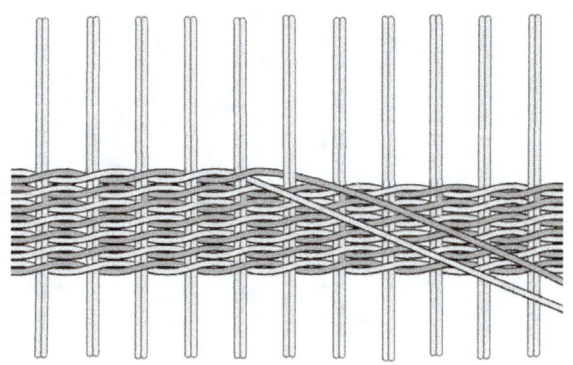

OPEN WORK

Open work is used to add variety to the surface texture of the basket by leaving the spokes exposed.(No reeds are woven across the spokes.)

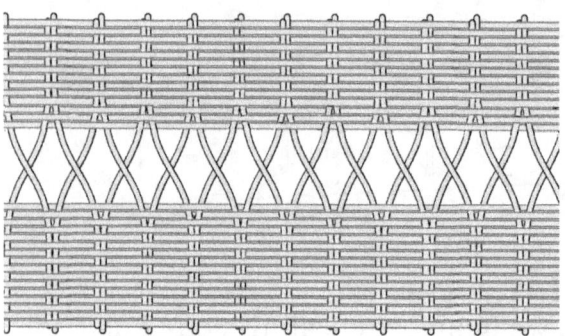

[STEP 1] Open Work.

End the weaving. Be sure that the end of the weaver is hidden.

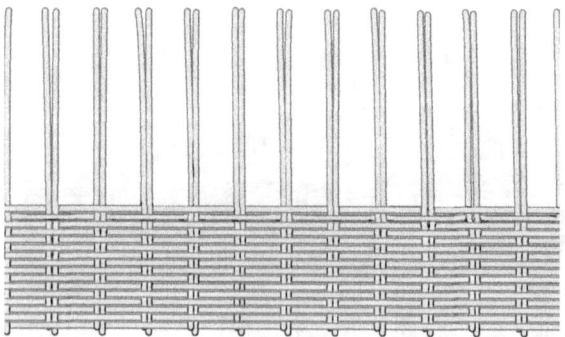

[STEP 2] Open Work.

Use a heavy cord to bind each pair of spokes together as shown. The left reed of each spoke is pulled to the left one spoke. The right reed of each spoke is pulled to the right one spoke. This forms a series of "X"s that will make up the texture of the open work.

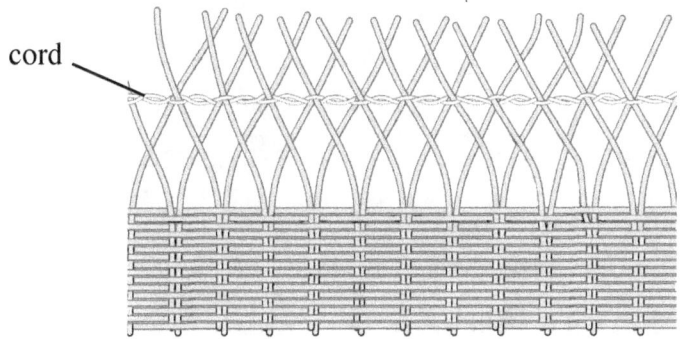

cord

[STEP 3] Open Work.

Insert a new weaver and weave 3 or 4 rounds. As the rounds of weaving progress, reestablish the spokes as parallel reeds.

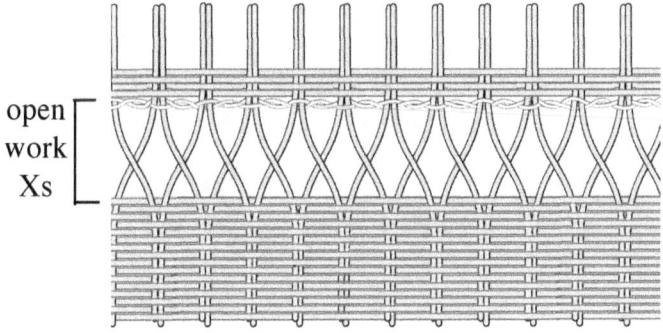

open work Xs

35

[STEP 4] Open Work.

Remove the cord and check the evenness of the width of the open work. Adjust if necessary.

check
width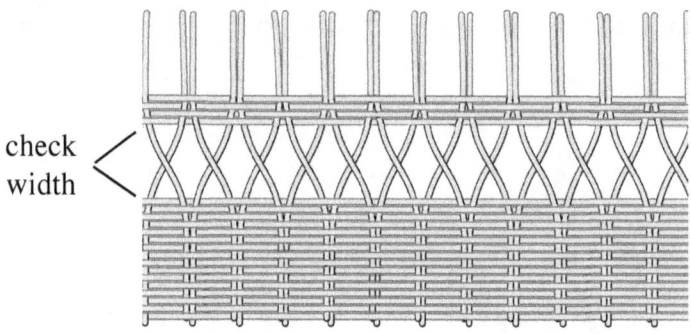

[STEP 5] Open Work.

Continue the weaving of the side of the basket.

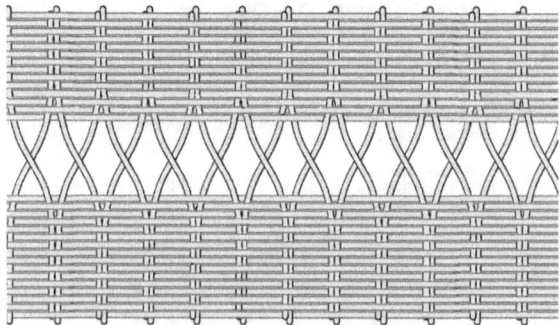

EXAMPLES

The photographs in this section illustrate the use of the various weaving methods and contrasting colors of reed.

Example 1: Single rod weave using contrasting colors.

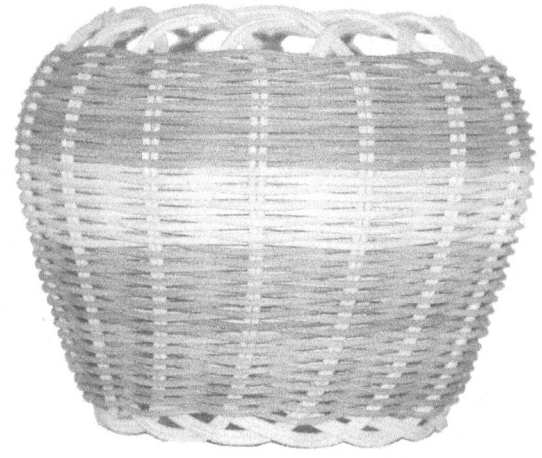

Example 2: Single rod weave using contrasting colors and open work.

single rod weave

open work

single rod weave

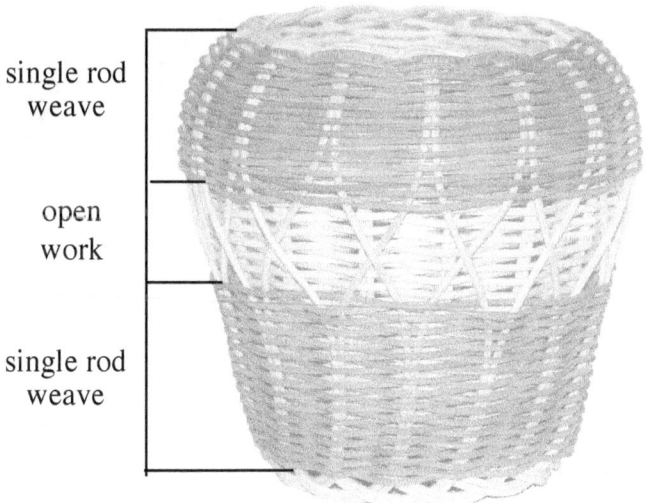

Example 3: Double rod over/under weave using contrasting colors.

2 dark
rods

1 dark and
1 light rod

2 light
rods

1 dark and
1 light rod

2 dark
rods

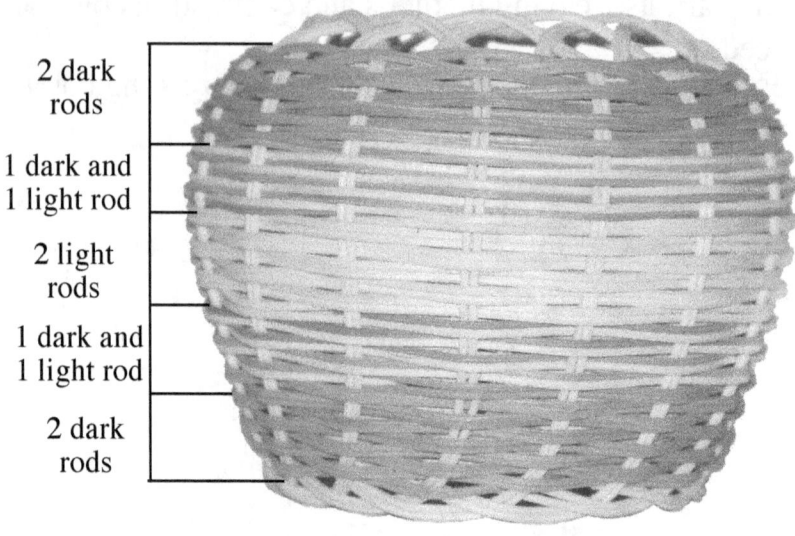

Example 4: Twining and single rod weaves using contrasting colors.

twining

single rod
weave

twining

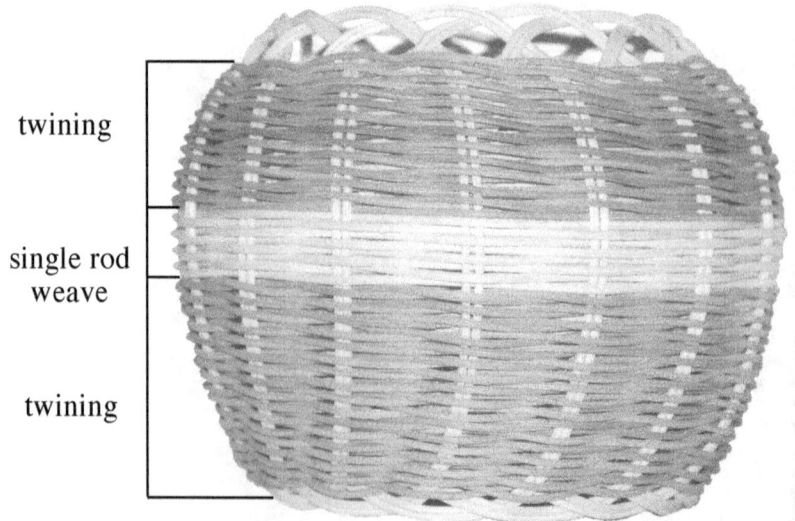

Example 5: Twining using contrasting colors.

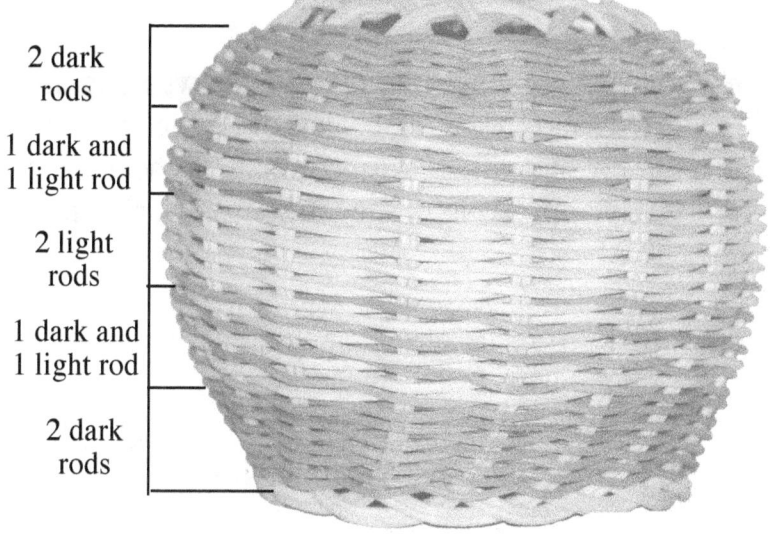

2 dark
rods

1 dark and
1 light rod

2 light
rods

1 dark and
1 light rod

2 dark
rods

GLOSSARY

dye pot --- a container used to dye the weaving material. **WARNING!** Because of the toxic nature of many dye products, once a pan has been used as a dye pot it should never be used for preparing food.

open work --- Space along the spokes where no weavers are used.

pliable --- Easily bent without breaking.

rod --- (1) A weaver. (2) A single reed used for weaving

round --- One complete row of weaving around the basket.

splice --- (1) The point at which two reeds meet. (2) The point at which a new reed is inserted into the work.

spoke --- A piece that forms the framework of the basket upon which the weavers are woven.

twining --- A weave in which two weavers cross each other as they weave around each spoke.

weaver ---The material that is used for the weaving.

INDEX